30 Day
Job Seeker's
Devotional

Monique E. Tuset, MSW

ISBN: 978-1-7323796-0-2

ACKNOWLEDGMENTS

God.
I want to thank God for blessing me with the ability to help so many people connect with their dreams. The Bible says "Commit to the Lord whatever you do and He will establish your plans (Proverbs 16:3 NIV)." I can truly say God exceeded my expectations in **every** area of my life after I began abiding by that Word!

Husband.
Te amo mi amor. Juan is the sweetest man I know and I am extremely blessed to have him as the love of my life. He is so patient and encouraging! I love you, best friend!

Eliana Tuset.
I love you so much baby girl. I'm excited to see how God is going to use you when you grow up!

In loving memory of my mama, Vivian Smith. She was the most encouraging and energetic cheerleader I had on my team. Now she is a part of my cloud of witnesses cheering me on from her heavenly home. (Hebrews 12:1). You will always be missed.

CONTENTS

HEY YOU!

I wrote this devotional with you in mind; actually, I had myself in mind as well. I know how it feels to search for jobs for hours, scouring website after website, emailing former professors and community members to inquire of open positions, and the fleeting thoughts of moving back to your hometown; where you're sure you can find something, but would have to forsake the quality of life you desire.

I also know the feelings of joy and excitement after receiving an email or a phone call to schedule an interview. You're pumped! You're excited! They're interested and you have a lead! I too have rushed frantically to Target or Marshalls to find the right outfit for the interview. I mean, you have to invest in yourself, right? The little splurge you did while shopping was nothing compared to the big check you're about to collect!

There are the jitters, nerves, sweat, and excitement on the day of your interview. You go in and nail it... other than the few questions you weren't expecting. You know it's your job! You begin "naming and claiming" the position on your route home! You believe God is going to bless you with the job of your dreams. Acting in faith, you map out your new route to work and determine how you'll say goodbye to your co-workers. You're relaxing in the new found peace you've stumbled into and then you get an email.

A generic email thanking you for applying but informs you that they've decided to pursue another candidate. You are BUMMED. WHAT? That job was mine! Who could be more qualified than me? Oh well. That job wasn't going to be that great anyways. It would've added 15 minutes to my current commute and the building had an odd smell. I didn't really.... Does this mean I have to go back to my current job tomorrow?

Does this mean my status remains "in transition" instead of "employed?"

If you can relate to any of this, I wrote this for you. The challenges of our faith can be rough in the job hunt process. I want to encourage you. The purpose of this devotional is to provide you with scripture, reflection on those scriptures, and space for you to write your reflection. I want you to use this devotional as a tool to stay motivated and encouraged through your journey.

Here's to happy reading and an empowered job search!

DAY 1
ALTER YOUR GAZE

SCRIPTURE READING FOR TODAY:
So we fix our eyes not on what is seen, but on what is unseen, since what is seen is temporary, but what is unseen is eternal.
2 Corinthians 4:18 NIV

APPLICATION OF SCRIPTURE:
When we're working our faith muscle in the job search process we want a job as the final result. Completing application after application day in and day out can become overwhelming and frustrating. However, God doesn't want you to focus on that. God wants you to focus on the fact that He's your provider and has all of your needs covered. Situations of need make you more dependent upon the one who can provide for you. Total dependence on God is good. It seems hard now, but it is truly working for your good.

The scripture above is taken from a larger passage of Corinthians where Paul is sharing the struggles of ministry, but ends it by making his audience aware that it's all worth it.

So for you, there may be struggles at the moment, but it will be worth it if you stay the course. I know you can't see your job right now, but understand that this state is only temporary. Meditate on your future job and how God will get the glory out of your job search process.

TODAY'S AFFIRMATION:
The job God has for me is looking for me. I do not have to stress about employment. My Father in heaven already has it covered.

ADDITIONAL SCRIPTURES FOR MEDITATION: Philippians 4:7; Philippians 4:19

THOUGHTS & REFLECTIONS:

What have I focused on in my job search? What is something practical I can implement that will shift my focus and alter my gaze?

DAY 2
BLESSED LEADERS

SCRIPTURE READING FOR TODAY:

Then I will give you shepherds after my own heart, who will lead you with knowledge and understanding.
Jeremiah 3:15 NIV

APPLICATION OF SCRIPTURE:

Sometimes former experiences with horrible bosses can cause anxiety about starting a new position. A terrible experience with a boss or a supervisor can make you feel wary about trusting a new boss.

Today's reading reflects God encouraging His people and informing them that He will send shepherds to take care of them. This is applicable to the job search as you trust that God will bless you with a supervisor that will lead you correctly and make your job enjoyable.

TODAY'S AFFIRMATION:

My new supervisor will love God and will be the best supervisor for me. They will challenge me to be better and will communicate in a manner that is most helpful to me. I trust God to have the right person in the position for me.

ADDITIONAL SCRIPTURE FOR MEDITATION: Psalms 37:5

THOUGHTS & REFLECTIONS:

What bad experiences with former supervisors still worry me? What is preventing me from trusting God that my next supervisor will be my best supervisor?

DAY 3
ESTABLISHED BY THE LORD

SCRIPTURE READING FOR TODAY:

Commit to the Lord whatever you do, and he will establish your plans. *Proverbs 16:3 NIV*

APPLICATION OF SCRIPTURE:

Proverbs 16:3 is one of the scriptures that guides my life. It's significant to me because as an action-oriented person, sometimes my goals get ahead of God. However, this scripture reminds me to slow my roll, consult with God, and follow His leading.

Commit your job search to Him daily. Seek God for what websites you should visit, who to contact for an informational interview, and what positions you should apply to. When you allow God to lead your process, He will ensure that you will be successful in all that you do.

My great-grandmother always said, "let Jesus lead you, and you won't go wrong." I encourage you to be led by Jesus. He knows what He's doing!

TODAY'S AFFIRMATION:

I'm not wandering through this job search unadvised. God is ordering my steps and has blessed my process because I have consulted with him. This job search is blessed!

ADDITIONAL SCRIPTURE FOR MEDITATION: Psalms 37:23

THOUGHTS & REFLECTIONS:

What areas of my job search do I need to commit to God? What have I tried to do on my own?

DAY 4
NEVER CHANGING

SCRIPTURE READING FOR TODAY:

Jesus Christ is the same yesterday and today and forever.
Hebrews 13:8 NIV

APPLICATION OF SCRIPTURE:

Has God ever done anything for you? One thing? If He has *before*, He will do it again! Why? Because God is the same yesterday, today, and forever!

If God has ever worked a miracle in your life, don't think He's run out of His miracle-working power. God is immutable and He's excited to bless you! God is able to bless us according to our level of faith.

If you sincerely can't think of anytime God has come through for you, I encourage you to ask Him to increase your faith. The job search process is not too hard for God. It's an easy thing for Him to do!

TODAY'S AFFIRMATION:

I know God loves me! I know God cares about me! If God did it for me before, He will do it for me again!

ADDITIONAL SCRIPTURE FOR MEDITATION: Acts 3:16

THOUGHTS & REFLECTIONS:

What are five miracles/things God has done in my life? What is preventing me from thinking He won't do it again?

DAY 5
STAY PRAYERFUL

SCRIPTURE READING FOR TODAY:
Devote yourselves to prayer, being watchful and thankful.
Colossians 4:2 NIV

APPLICATION OF SCRIPTURE:
Today's scripture is profound and provides great context and perspective for the job search. Most times we think we should engulf ourselves in our goal(s) and ignore distractions to avoid wasting time. However, for most things in life, if you commit to this scripture, and truly focus on prayer above the other things, you will be successful.

What does it mean to devote yourself to prayer? Does it mean you have to pray 24/7? No. However, it does mean you're praying more than once or twice a week. Think of what you're currently devoted to. Are you a huge sports fan? Do you always watch when your team is playing? Are you a YouTube fanatic who watches videos all of the time? Think about the energy and excitement you have when you are participating in those things and consider prayer the same way.

TODAY'S AFFIRMATION:
I am devoted to prayer over everything else in my life. Prayer is vital to my success.

ADDITIONAL SCRIPTURES FOR MEDITATION: 1 Thessalonians 5:16-18

THOUGHTS & REFLECTIONS:

What are some things I can cut from my schedule to devote more time to prayer?

DAY 6
SUBMITTING TO TRUST

SCRIPTURE READING FOR TODAY:
Trust in the Lord with all your heart and lean not on your own understanding; in all your ways submit to him, and he will make your paths straight.
Proverbs 3:5-6 NIV

APPLICATION OF SCRIPTURE:
Today's scripture is probably one of the most popular scriptures as it relates to encouraging folks to increase their trust in God. Society prizes independence so much that releasing their will to God is incredibly hard for many people.

We are instructed to trust in God and not our own understanding. This means to neglect how we feel naturally, and accept what God is doing spiritually.

This scripture is also good for those searching for their God-given purpose and vocation. God will direct us to the right paths as we continue to submit to him. His word is a lamp unto our feet and a light unto our path.

What are you waiting for? It's time to trust God like never before!

TODAY'S AFFIRMATION:
I am a faith-filled person. I have the faith to walk on water! I will operate in the faith I have from today until I leave this earth!

ADDITIONAL SCRIPTURE FOR MEDITATION: Psalms 119:105

THOUGHTS & REFLECTIONS:

How will increasing my faith benefit me? What can I do to build my faith? (Hint: Romans 10:17)

DAY 7
IT'S ALL GOD

SCRIPTURE READING FOR TODAY:

You may say to yourself, "My power and the strength of my hands have produced this wealth for me." But remember the Lord your God, for it is He who gives you the ability to produce wealth, and so confirms His covenant, which He swore to your ancestors, as it is today.
Deuteronomy 8:17-18 NIV

APPLICATION OF SCRIPTURE:

Have you ever heard the phrase "it's all good!"? In place of that phrase, you should begin saying "It's all God!" Why? Because unfortunately, when people reach the blessings they strived for, becoming accomplished, they forget about the moments of vulnerability and desperation they had prior to success. They forget it was truly a miracle from God that got them where they are today.

This isn't a 21st or 22nd-century concept. This was happening centuries ago. Our scripture today points out an ancient flaw we have to guard ourselves against. We have to remember that everything we have, everything we've done, and everything we are going to do is because of God.

When we acknowledge that it's God and not ourselves, we worship God and bring Him glory. That then points others towards God. So remember, it's all God! It's not us!

TODAY'S AFFIRMATION:

I will give God glory in all that I accomplish. I know I can do nothing without His power.

ADDITIONAL SCRIPTURE FOR MEDITATION: John 15:8

THOUGHTS & REFLECTIONS:

Am I guilty of taking God's glory at times? How will I make sure that all glory is given to Him in the future?

DAY 8
BLESSINGS AND PROSPERITY

SCRIPTURE READING FOR TODAY:
Blessed are all who fear the Lord, who walk in obedience to Him. You will eat the fruit of your labor; blessings and prosperity will be yours. *Psalms 128:1-2 NIV*

APPLICATION OF SCRIPTURE:
A surefire way to be blessed is by serving the Lord Jesus. Of course, we see others in society who are far from serving Jesus while enjoying nice things, but we have a promise. The promise that believers in Jesus Christ have is explained in today's passage. Blessings and prosperity will be ours.

It is impossible not to be blessed when we're walking with Jesus. It is impossible for goodness and mercy not to follow us when we're with Christ Jesus.

During your job search know this, blessings and prosperity can't stay away from you. You are dripping in the favor of God. You will be blessed in all that you do! The job that will be the biggest blessing for you in this season, at this moment, while you're at this stage in life, will come to you.

TODAY'S AFFIRMATION:
I have an abundance of God's favor on my life. I believe blessings and prosperity are mine. I'm obedient to God and I will continue to reap goodness and mercy.

ADDITIONAL SCRIPTURE FOR MEDITATION: Psalms 23:6

THOUGHTS & REFLECTIONS:

Do I really believe blessings and prosperity are mine?

DAY 9
WORKING FOR GOOD

SCRIPTURE READING FOR TODAY:
And we know that in all things God works for the good of those who love him, who have been called according to his purpose.
Romans 8:28 NIV

APPLICATION OF SCRIPTURE:
Today's scripture is such a beautiful one. It's one of the many verses that provides an extremely high dose of faith if you allow yourself to absorb it.

It promises that God will use everything for our good. No, it doesn't say that God causes the bad things to happen, but it *does* say that He will use them for our good! What a wonderful promise!

The interviews you bombed, the job you were fired from, the unfair treatment you received, even the ridicule of being unemployed, God will use it all. But there is a caveat; you have to love God and have been called to Him. So if you haven't accepted the Lord Jesus as your personal savior, give Him a try so that you can reap the benefits of powerful scriptures like these.

TODAY'S AFFIRMATION:
I am a recipient of God's good works in my life because I love Him. I have faith to know that all things will work for my good.

ADDITIONAL SCRIPTURE FOR MEDITATION: Psalms 90:17

THOUGHTS & REFLECTIONS:

Do I believe that God will work everything in my life for my good?

DAY 10
REMAINING IN CHRIST

SCRIPTURE READING FOR TODAY:

Remain in me, as I also remain in you. No branch can bear fruit by itself; it must remain in the vine. Neither can you bear fruit unless you remain in me.
John 15:4 NIV

APPLICATION OF SCRIPTURE:

Today's scripture provides great encouragement to stay in the way of the Lord. It helps us realize we will be fruitless apart from Christ. Imagine a budding orange. How bizarre would it be if the orange decided to hop off the tree and try to finish its development without the nutrients from the tree? That would be insane!

This scripture parallels us to a fruit or vegetable that needs a vine. We will not flourish if we attempt independence and separate from God. We will fail in most of what we do. Of course, there are others who don't believe in Christ but do well in life. However, just like the orange that is not fully grown, they will not reach their full God-given potential.

Let's work to remain in Christ, continuing to bear fruit and reach our God-given potential.

TODAY'S AFFIRMATION:

I will remain in Christ because I want to reach my full potential. I will bear fruit because I will remain in Christ.

ADDITIONAL SCRIPTURE FOR MEDITATION: Hebrews 6:19

THOUGHTS & REFLECTIONS:

How does it feel to know I will bear fruit in Christ?

DAY 11
REST IN CHRIST

SCRIPTURE READING FOR TODAY:

Come to me, all you who are weary and burdened, and I will give you rest.
Matthew 11:28 NIV

APPLICATION OF SCRIPTURE:

You're in for a treat today. Our scripture application is by my sweet husband, Juan Tuset. Resting in Christ is a topic that Juan has received an abundance of revelation about, and he is excited to share some of it!

Juan Tuset

This is a pretty familiar passage for most of us. But I'd like to expound on a concept in this verse that, perhaps, you've never noticed before. Jesus isn't just giving a friendly invitation. This is an imperative sentence. Meaning, Jesus is *commanding* us to come to *Him* for rest. We're often tempted to run every-which-way to take a load off or get some release from all of the stress we're under. Some overeat, some binge on TV, some pour over social media for hours on end, or some of us do things that seem wholesome like spending time with our family.

However, the Savior makes it clear that true rest can only be found in Him. There is no substitute for the soul-rest we find in Christ. So remember, you will only get rest in Christ. Get to Him as quickly as possible.

TODAY'S AFFIRMATION:

Lord, you provide all of my needs. I come to you for rest. In you, my entire being is refreshed.

ADDITIONAL SCRIPTURES FOR MEDITATION: Psalms 4:8; Matthew 11:28-30; Psalms 23:2

THOUGHTS & REFLECTIONS:

What sources have I been running to for rest? What changes will I make after today?

DAY 12
KEEP CALM AND STAY CONFIDENT

SCRIPTURE READING FOR TODAY:
So do not throw away your confidence; it will be richly rewarded. You need to persevere so that when you have done the will of God, you will receive what he has promised.
Hebrews 10:35-36 NIV

APPLICATION OF SCRIPTURE:
It becomes more than discouraging when you're deep in your job search and it seems like there are zero leads. Especially as a believer. The scriptures tell us that our Father in heaven owns all the cattle on a thousand hills, so of course, He can give us the job we really want, right? Of course He can; but because of the way we are wired, when we want something, we want it immediately! "I want it, and I want it now!"

However, today's scripture it is a gentle reminder to keep our confidence in Christ and persevere so that we receive our promise.

Your job is coming! Your job is near! Stay focused! Stay encouraged! Keep your confidence up! Rest in the assurance that God has it covered and loves you more than you know.

TODAY'S AFFIRMATION:
I will keep my confidence in Christ regardless of what things look like. I will hang in there until I receive my promise.

ADDITIONAL SCRIPTURES FOR MEDITATION: Psalmss 50:10-11

THOUGHTS & REFLECTIONS:

What are some practical things I can do to keep my confidence in Christ? Am I really assured that He will provide a job for me?

DAY 13
WAIT FOR IT

SCRIPTURE READING FOR TODAY:
When God made his promise to Abraham, since there was no one greater for him to swear by, he swore by himself, saying, "I will surely bless you and give you many descendants." And so after waiting patiently, Abraham received what was promised.
Hebrews 6:13-15 NIV

APPLICATION OF SCRIPTURE:
If you have never heard about Abraham, I encourage you to research him. Most of the Old Testament focuses on descendants from his lineage and his life is truly interesting.

Today's reading highlights a momentous time in Abraham's life. Abraham and his wife Sarah did not have any children. They were 99 and 90 years old. God promised him that Sarah would give birth to a son and that his descendants would be as numerous as the stars in the sky. That was a huge promise. It seems almost ridiculous when we think about it naturally, but God operates in the realm of the spirit. He is eternal, so time and age don't matter to Him.

The key to Abraham receiving the promise was patience. Was he always patient? No. At one point he took matters into his own hands and attempted to help God make the promise happen (see Genesis 15). When his plan failed, Abraham turned back to God and decided that being patient was a better option. After Abraham changed his heart, God fulfilled the promise and Isaac was born!

TODAY'S AFFIRMATION:
I will patiently wait on God to fulfill His promises.

ADDITIONAL SCRIPTURES FOR MEDITATION: Genesis 21:1-6

THOUGHTS & REFLECTIONS:

What have I tried to do to "help" God manifest His promises in my life? How has that worked out so far? What will I do differently?

DAY 14
I AM GOING TO ASK

SCRIPTURE READING FOR TODAY:
Ask and it will be given to you; seek and you will find; knock and the door will be opened to you. For everyone who asks receives; the one who seeks finds; and to the one who knocks the door will be opened. *Matthew 7:7-8 NIV*

APPLICATION OF SCRIPTURE:
Have you ever heard the saying "a closed mouth doesn't get fed"? It came to mind when I read today's scripture. The quote means if you don't ask for what you want, you won't get it.

How many of us have started job searches without asking God for specific things we want in our next position? Are we just saying "God, give me a job"? Are we just asking God to provide for us? When we pray, God gets the most glory from answering specific prayers that challenge us, although they are easy to God. Sometimes we play it safe and water down what we really want from fear that God won't deliver our desire.

Today's scripture encourages us to ask and it will be given! God is waiting for the request! He's waiting for your request! There's a story in the Bible where Jesus encountered a blind man and asked the blind man what he wanted. Of course, it seemed obvious. The blind man wanted to see, but God waited until the man responded before He worked the miracle.

Are you waiting for your dream job because you haven't asked God for it?

TODAY'S AFFIRMATION:
I know that my God is big! I will begin to pray bigger prayers!

ADDITIONAL SCRIPTURE FOR MEDITATION: Mark 10 :51

THOUGHTS & REFLECTIONS:

What do I want God to do for me?

DAY 15
MANAGING MONEY

SCRIPTURE READING FOR TODAY:

Whoever can be trusted with very little can also be trusted with much, and whoever is dishonest with very little will also be dishonest with much. So if you have not been trustworthy in handling worldly wealth, who will trust you with true riches?
Luke 16:10-11 NIV

APPLICATION OF SCRIPTURE:

Have you ever prayed for a bigger salary? For just a little more money to make some major financial moves you've been thinking about? Well, to gauge if you're actually ready for a higher salary, examine how you're managing your current salary.

Do you budget? Do you really budget? Do you know where your money is going opposed to wondering where it went? Are you a good steward of your money? Today's scripture challenges us with the way we manage our money. God actually relates the way we manage our finances to our worthiness to be trusted with true riches in Christ. That's pretty big!

Now that we have this charge let's become the best stewards over our finances that we can be; so that we can not only be blessed with bigger salaries but also with the true riches in Christ Jesus.

TODAY'S AFFIRMATION:

I know where my money goes. I am a good steward of my money. I am mature enough to handle the riches of Christ Jesus.

ADDITIONAL SCRIPTURE FOR MEDITATION: Matthew 6:21

THOUGHTS & REFLECTIONS:

What are some immediate changes I can make with my spending habits to manage my salary better? How will I hold myself accountable for this adjustment?

DAY 16
WORKING FOR GOD

SCRIPTURE READING FOR TODAY:
Whatever you do, work at it with all your heart, as working for the Lord, not for human masters.
Colossians 3:23 NIV

APPLICATION OF SCRIPTURE:
Have you ever been in sports practice and stopped the activity you were instructed to do when the coach turned their head or left the room? As a former basketball player, there are many wall-sits and sprints I never completed.

For those of you who have never played sports, what about work? Do you find yourself browsing the internet, or doing whatever you like, quickly switching your screen to something different as soon as someone walks into the room?

Well, today's reading is convicting for us all! The scripture challenges us to do everything we're supposed to do as if we are working for God opposed to humans. Guess what! God is omnipresent. He is always with us. So let's take this charge to operate with a spirit of excellence in everything we do!

TODAY'S AFFIRMATION:
I will work as if God is watching me. I will be excellent in the things I do for the glory of God.

ADDITIONAL SCRIPTURES FOR MEDITATION: Psalms 37:4-5

THOUGHTS & REFLECTIONS:

What areas can I improve to showcase excellence in my work?

DAY 17
#HARDWORK

SCRIPTURE READING FOR TODAY:

She sets about her work vigorously; her arms are strong for her tasks. *Proverbs 31:17 NIV*

APPLICATION OF SCRIPTURE:

Proverbs 31 is one of the best-known passages for highlighting a hard-working woman. It highlights how she cares for others, how savvy she is, how thrifty she is, and most importantly, her wisdom when it comes to work ethic.

It's important to approach your job search with a strong work ethic. Job searching can be exhausting, but you don't want laziness or apathy to set in. It could lead to giving up on your goals. You must have stamina in your search process and be disciplined in your approach. The Bible gives us the example of the woman in Proverbs 31 for how much, when empowered by God, a woman can do.

Be encouraged! You've got this!

TODAY'S AFFIRMATION:

I'm not afraid of hard work. I'm ready to tackle this job search process and I will not back down or settle for less.

ADDITIONAL SCRIPTURE FOR MEDITATION: Psalms 90:17

THOUGHTS & REFLECTIONS:

What is my job search strategy? Do I feel exhausted? If so, how can I recharge and get back in the game?

DAY 18
FULL OF HOPE

SCRIPTURE READING FOR TODAY:
May the God of hope fill you with all joy and peace as you trust in him, so that you may overflow with hope by the power of the Holy Spirit.
Romans 15:13 NIV

APPLICATION OF SCRIPTURE:
The job search process can sometimes be void of hope. It may seem that nothing you try is working and you could begin to lose hope. Especially if you've been in the search for more than 6 months.

Have you ever felt like this? You've applied for way more positions than you've had interviews and when you had an interview, it didn't result in a position.

The verse for today is to encourage you in the Lord and remind you of the God that sits on the throne. He is a loving God who is ready to pour all of His hope into you today!

TODAY'S AFFIRMATION:
Hopelessness is no longer my best friend. I am full of hope and joy! As I continue to trust in God, my hope will be renewed and refreshed.

ADDITIONAL SCRIPTURE FOR MEDITATION: Nehemiah 8:10

THOUGHTS & REFLECTIONS:

How does it feel to know God fills people with hope? Has it been difficult to receive this hope?

DAY 19
YOU ARE ENOUGH

SCRIPTURE READING FOR TODAY:
But the Lord said to me, "Do not say, 'I am too young.' You must go to everyone I send you to and say whatever I command you. Do not be afraid of them, for I am with you and will rescue you," declares the Lord.
Jeremiah 1:7-8 NIV

APPLICATION OF SCRIPTURE:
Sometimes we shortchange ourselves during job searches because we don't feel we have enough experience. Have you ever considered the fact that God is the one who prepares you and equips you for every position you'll ever have?

Stop telling yourself you don't have enough this or that. Just go for it! God is with you and has your back. You get 0% of the positions you don't apply for! Why not at least try?

Sometimes an employer is willing to take a candidate that is teachable and can grow to a new level. Be willing to put yourself in the running for positions you don't necessarily qualify for and see how God works!

TODAY'S AFFIRMATION:
I am enough. I have what I need. I am going for the position I really want. My experience and degree will no longer hold me back. I will allow God to be God in my life.

ADDITIONAL SCRIPTURE FOR MEDITATION: Ephesians 2:10

THOUGHTS & REFLECTION:

What positions do I really want? What position qualifications have I allowed to prevent me from applying for those positions? How can I tailor my documents to get my foot into an interview?

DAY 20
GOD'S APPROVAL

SCRIPTURE READING FOR TODAY:

And may the Lord our God show us his approval and make our efforts successful. Yes, make our efforts successful!
Psalms 90:17 NIV

APPLICATION OF SCRIPTURE:

Sometimes we seek the approval of co-workers, supervisors, and others at work. We must keep in mind that our desire should be to win God's approval so that our work will become successful. In a later devotional, we will discuss your definition of success. We see here that our efforts are made successful when we receive God's approval on our projects.

How is this applicable? Start with prayer. Ask God to help you complete the tasks He has for you when you arrive to work. Spoiler alert! Sometimes this prayer will have you ministering the Word of God to a co-worker or praying for an hour during your lunch break. You never know! Nonetheless, this is a great practical step for you to take when you desire God's approval on your work. Don't feel that it's a competition; as if the only way to win approval is by completing a thousand tasks at work or completing 50+ job applications per day. Ask God to lead you in the direction you should go before you apply for a job. Rely on Him and not your connections or networking ability.

TODAY'S AFFIRMATION:

I will seek God's approval so that my work will be successful.

ADDITIONAL SCRIPTURE FOR MEDITATION: Psalms 5:3

THOUGHTS & REFLECTIONS:

What new practice will I implement to win God's approval? How will I release pride in wanting to achieve success on my own?

DAY 21
A NEW THING

SCRIPTURE READING FOR TODAY:
See, the former things have taken place, and new things I declare; before they spring into being I announce them to you.
Isaiah 42:9 NIV

APPLICATION OF SCRIPTURE:
Sometimes the past likes to linger and prevent us from moving forward. I remember chatting with someone who was afraid of getting a job interview because of the dreaded question "so, why did you leave your last position"? This person was terminated from their previous position due to an ethical issue. They didn't know how to word the situation in a way they felt comfortable. They allowed the situation to haunt them for several years.

Our scripture for today reminds us that the past has happened, but God is getting ready to do a new thing! Don't allow the past to control your future. Allow God to rewrite your story.

TODAY'S AFFIRMATION:
I am a forward-thinker. I will not allow the thoughts of my past to prevent me from going forward. I am focused on my future success and my past will stay in the past where it belongs. I am a new person today. I am not the same as I was yesterday!

ADDITIONAL SCRIPTURES FOR MEDITATION: 2 Corinthians 5:17; Isaiah 43:18-19

THOUGHTS & REFLECTIONS:

What situation(s) have I allowed to hold me back from future success? What am I not presently pursuing because of my past?

DAY 22
YOU HAVE NO IDEA

SCRIPTURE READING FOR TODAY:

However, as it is written: "What no eye has seen, what no ear has heard, and what no human mind has conceived" — the things God has prepared for those who love him.
1 Corinthians 2:9 NIV

APPLICATION OF SCRIPTURE:

Can you believe you have no idea what God wants to do in your life? You don't have a clue! God's thoughts are so far beyond ours that it's crazy! Isn't it exciting? Think about it, if it was up to you to plan how everything would go in your life, it wouldn't be as good as it could be. I can reflect on the last five years of my life and praise God for prayers He did not answer.

As you continue your job search, realize God has much more for you than you can plan right now. I know people often use the cliché "everything happens for a reason;" replace it with the Word. Recite 1 Corinthians 2:9, "...no human mind has conceived the things God has prepared for those who love Him."

TODAY'S AFFIRMATION:

I am excited to see the incredible things God is going to do in my life.

ADDITIONAL SCRIPTURE FOR MEDITATION: Ephesians 3:20

THOUGHTS & REFLECTIONS:

What are the biggest things I can think of God doing for me right now? Do I really believe God can do something better than that? If not, what is blocking my faith?

DAY 23
WHAT IS SUCCESS?

SCRIPTURE READING FOR TODAY:
Brothers and sisters, I do not consider myself yet to have taken hold of it. But one thing I do: Forgetting what is behind and straining toward what is ahead, I press on toward the goal to win the prize for which God has called me heavenward in Christ Jesus.
Philippians 3:13-14 NIV

APPLICATION OF SCRIPTURE:
Have you considered if what you're searching for, the success you're after, actually lines up with how you define success? Is this your vision of success or is it society's vision? Have you taken the time to jot down your goals and your definition of success? If not, take time to do that today.

As you're considering your definition of success, how does it line up with your God-given potential? Do you feel your definition will glorify God or does it solely give you glory? Are you seeking these goals to win the approval or accolades of others?

Today's scripture ties into a discussion about success because we often allow our past failures to dictate our definition of success. The Word encourages us to forget the things that are behind us and press on towards the goal that God has called us to.

TODAY'S AFFIRMATION:
My definition of success gives glory to God. I will not allow my past to dictate how I see my future.

ADDITIONAL SCRIPTURES FOR MEDITATION: Psalms 37:23-24

THOUGHTS & REFLECTIONS:

What does success mean to me? Will this reveal my God-given potential?

DAY 24
GUARD YOUR HEART

SCRIPTURE READING FOR TODAY:

Above all else, guard your heart, for everything you do flows from it.
Proverbs 4:23 NIV

APPLICATION OF SCRIPTURE:

Regardless of how the need to search for a job came about, the situation can send dangerous messages to our hearts. Our hearts may become fearful, anxious, or even depressed when we reflect on the decisions and reasons for why we're here. Especially if we have been searching for a job for a long time.

We also have to guard our hearts from negative messages from our families and friends. They may not believe your job search is wise, they may continuously question your decisions, or they may make you feel bad for being unemployed or underemployed. You have to guard yourself from that.

The most practical way for you to guard your heart from negativity is by giving your heart to God. If you are a visual person, I encourage you to draw a heart on a piece of paper and hand it to God. God can protect your heart better than you can. He will ensure it is kept safe during this process.

TODAY'S AFFIRMATION:

I am committed to happiness and peace in my job search. I will not believe the lies of fear, anxiety, depression, or doubt that try to enter my heart.

ADDITIONAL SCRIPTURES FOR MEDITATION: Matthew 11:28-30; Psalms 4:8

THOUGHTS & REFLECTIONS:

In what ways has my heart feared in this job search? What other feelings has my heart felt? How will I guard myself?

DAY 25
KEEP BUILDING

SCRIPTURE READING FOR TODAY:
Tobiah the Ammonite, who was at his side, said, "What they are building—even a fox climbing up on it would break down their wall of stones!"
Nehemiah 4:3 NIV

APPLICATION OF SCRIPTURE:
Have you ever been in the process of building something positive for your life and felt like negative people continued to bring you down? Has it seemed as if every step you've taken was met with a sly comment about how you should have done it differently?

In the passage above, we read a negative comment someone made about Nehemiah and his people as they were building a wall to protect their city. The negative people around them, merely spectators and critics in the process, continually tried to stop them from building. What did Nehemiah and his people continue to do? They kept building!

So, be encouraged! If you're building your empire or making career moves to set yourself up for your future and it seems that negativity is all around, KEEP BUILDING!

TODAY'S AFFIRMATION:
I am a mega-builder. God and I will build an amazing future for my career. My time of being unemployed or searching for a better position will conclude soon.

ADDITIONAL SCRIPTURE FOR MEDITATION: Isaiah 54:17

THOUGHTS & REFLECTIONS:

What negative people or comments have affected my building process? What are positive things I can believe instead of their negativity?

DAY 26
LIVING IN PEACE

SCRIPTURE READING FOR TODAY:
Make every effort to live in peace with everyone and to be holy; without holiness no one will see the Lord.
Hebrews 12:14 NIV

APPLICATION OF SCRIPTURE:
Thankfully, I have been very blessed throughout my career to have great co-workers. However, I know this isn't a reality for everyone. Sometimes, horrible co-workers may push you to desire a new job.

The scripture above places the responsibility in the workplace on us. It is our job to do everything we can to live in peace with people around us. It's also our job to be an example of what it means to live in Christ Jesus.

If you're not a believer yet, I encourage you to surrender your life to Christ. He loves you more than you know! After you become a believer in Jesus Christ, He will empower you with His Holy Spirit. The Holy Spirit will make today's scripture easier.

TODAY'S AFFIRMATION:
The Holy Spirit empowers me to be in peace with everyone in my workplace. I am a peaceful person and I am holy.

ADDITIONAL SCRIPTURE FOR MEDITATION: 1 Corinthians 3:16

THOUGHTS & REFLECTIONS:

What has been difficult about living in peace this year? How will I be more intentional about living in peace?

DAY 27
FOCUS ON THE TRUTH

SCRIPTURE READING FOR TODAY:
Finally, brothers and sisters, whatever is true, whatever is noble, whatever is right, whatever is pure, whatever is lovely, whatever is admirable—if anything is excellent or praiseworthy—think about such things.
Philippians 4:8 NIV

APPLICATION OF SCRIPTURE:
You know the feeling you get when you really want something but you don't get it? It doesn't feel good, does it?

After being rejected, we are often visited by negative inner thoughts that say things like "you won't ever find a job; you're not good at interviewing; you don't have enough skills; you should just stop trying."

Guess what! Our father, God, knew those negative thoughts would come beforehand. He sent us a reminder in today's scripture. God wants us to focus on what's true. Is it true that you're not good enough? No. That's a lie. Sure, you may not have been the best fit for that company at the time, but you are good enough.

Let's focus on the truth. What does God say about you?

TODAY'S AFFIRMATION:
Today I will focus on the truth. I am who God says I am. My situation is what *God* says my situation is.

ADDITIONAL SCRIPTURES FOR MEDITATION: 3 John 1:4; Psalms 139:14

THOUGHTS & REFLECTIONS:

What untruths have I allowed my mind to entertain? What is the truth about those things?

DAY 28
REJOICING WHEN IT HURTS

SCRIPTURE READING FOR TODAY:
Rejoice always, pray continually, give thanks in all circumstances; for this is God's will for you in Christ Jesus.
1 Thessalonians 5:16-18 NIV

APPLICATION OF SCRIPTURE:
You get a notification from your email app and realize it's from the company you interviewed with a few weeks ago. You are filled with excitement and anticipation. You open the email, and the first few lines take your breath away.

"Dear applicant (they didn't even use your name),
Thank you for applying to our company. The competition was tough and although you were competitive, we have selected a more qualified candidate."

Silence.

Your mind is racing a mile a minute. You begin to hear negative thoughts in your mind. Discouragement starts to set in. The scripture reading for today is vital at this critical moment. Here is where our faith is built. We rejoice in the decision from the company, give thanks to God, accept it, and move on. We don't allow rejection to set in because our trust is rooted in the Father's love for us.

TODAY'S AFFIRMATION:
I will give thanks to God regardless of the circumstance! God's will for my life is what's best for my life!

ADDITIONAL SCRIPTURES FOR MEDITATION: Jeremiah 29:11; Proverbs 3:5-6

THOUGHTS & REFLECTIONS:

How have I dealt with rejection in the past? What will I commit to doing differently?

DAY 29
STAY ON GUARD

SCRIPTURE READING FOR TODAY:
When anxiety was great within me, your consolation brought me joy.
Psalms 94:19 NIV

APPLICATION OF SCRIPTURE:
Known as the silent killer, stress is incredibly dangerous to your body, especially your heart. If you are currently unemployed, stress may try to be your best friend, but you can't let it. You must guard your heart. To guard against stress, it is recommended to get involved in self-care activities. Self-care is simply doing activities that are enjoyable to you without causing more harm to your body or situation.

Meditation is a self-care technique that many people use regardless of their religious beliefs. As believers, we're instructed several times to meditate on the Word. We are not to allow the Word to depart from our hearts.

We have to stay on guard against stress in the natural. What are some spiritual things we need to stay on guard against? We need to be watchful for oppression from the enemy, condemnation, depression, rejection, laziness, complacency, and anything else that shakes our faith and hope in Jesus.

TODAY'S AFFIRMATION:
I'm on guard. My heart is protected. I will meditate on the Word of God daily.

ADDITIONAL SCRIPTURE FOR MEDITATION: Joshua 1:8

THOUGHTS & REFLECTIONS:

What are some of my favorite scriptures? Where can I put these scriptures to make it easier for me to meditate on them?

DAY 30
#NOFEAR

SCRIPTURE READING FOR TODAY:
So do not fear, for I am with you; do not be dismayed, for I am your God. I will strengthen you and help you; I will uphold you with my righteous right hand.
Isaiah 41:10 NIV

APPLICATION OF SCRIPTURE:
Have you ever watched how small children relax and rest in their parents' arms? They don't seem to have a care in the world. They feel safe and peaceful. That's exactly how our Father wants us to feel. However, when we attempt to do everything on our own, we become overwhelmed and frustrated. It feels as if God has left us hanging.

The Word reminds us that God is with us. God will strengthen, help, and uphold us. Allow yourself to rest in the assurance that God has everything under control. You are well taken care of.

TODAY'S AFFIRMATION:
I will no longer allow society to force me from God's presence. I will rest in the confidence that I have in Him. I know God has taken care of everything and all I need is in Him.

ADDITIONAL SCRIPTURES FOR MEDITATION: 1 John 5:14-15

THOUGHTS & REFLECTIONS:

What ways have I partnered with fear during my job search?
What will I do when I sense fear is in the driver's seat?

ABOUT THE AUTHOR

Monique Tuset considers herself a dream connector. Her personal mission in business and life is to help make goals attainable. One way she does so is by utilizing her skills to help connect individuals with their career goals.

She currently resides in North Carolina and is married to her best friend, Juan. They have one child, a beautiful daughter. Monique has two degrees from The University of North Carolina at Chapel Hill. She is a believer in Jesus Christ and loves God with her whole heart.

To find out what Monique is up to, please check out her website: www.moniquetuset.com.

www.ingramcontent.com/pod-product-compliance
Lightning Source LLC
LaVergne TN
LVHW021546080426
835509LV00019B/2875